80 Shades of Red

Irene Jones Coatta

ISBN-13: 978-1717023131
ISBN-10: 1717023134

DEDICATION

To my family and all the 'men' in my life.'

For my 'Lee Jo' with love

Mom

Contents

1
"Fly Away"

Why would I want to *'FLY AWAY'* with such an interesting fun life ahead to experience? Perhaps you will determine the reason as you read my memoir?

Believe it or not, I really did do all the things you are about to read!

As a little girl I had always wanted to 'fly like a bird!' I used to dream that I could just fly simply by flapping my arms and become airborne then fly wherever I wished to go! When I was young I climbed up on our steep barn roof, with my umbrella tucked under my arm, to show my twin sister that I really could fly. She cried, *'No Irene, you'll get hurt!'* *"Just watch me I hollered back to her"*, as I quickly pummeled to the ground when the umbrella inverted!

Not to have my desires squashed, I got one of our bed sheets and tied two ends together on each side then; again, I climbed the barn roof for my next attempt. I recall that I did have a brief 'puff of a parasail effect' before the knots became loose and, as before, I ended up face down on the terra firma!

So now I am endeavoring to *'fly'* into the art of writing my memoir!

La Troisieme' is the so-called 'third age'–from age sixty-five to one hundred years or more. I am now enjoying the 'third-age' of life and chose to record my interesting life to-date for my family and friends.

In many ways, writing a memoir is like painting. You slap some words on a blank canvas – take a few steps back, look at how they're coming together, and then refine things a little further. That step back is retrospection. Writing is one of the most painful of the ARTS – exposing ones thoughts, weakness, strengths, etc. Honesty is not only a gift to other people – it is a gift to you.

Too much vital history has been lost – just because people did NOT record events while they were alive. After all, words, photos and paintings are the only sure weapon one has against oblivion.

Some of the characters' names have been changed to protect their privacy and my 'neck'!

II
Meet My Family

Not wanting to sound too egotistical as the narrator of my memoir I do realize I should be consistent throughout the story, from beginning to the end, as to the 'I-We voice'. However, my memoir starts at the beginning of my life and my story will start in the 'plural' voice because I am a twin.

Ilene and I were born on Sunday, August 16, 1931 at Owen Taylor Hospital in Auburn, Washington State. Our Daddy used to tell us that he found us hanging in a 'gunny sack' on the barn wall when he went out to milk the cows. We sort of believed him when we were little. Below is a photo taken of me and Ilene at about the age of six-months? The photo shows us in our high chairs on the front porch of our family home at the twenty-seven acre dairy farm where we joined our parents along with three other siblings.

Twins born August 16, 1931
(l) Irene Ines Jones (r) Ilene Agnes Jones

Our older siblings, Alice, age ten, Betty Mignonette, age seven, and our brother, Jack, age five, all attended our Wabash Presbyterian Church for the Sunday School service where they proudly announced the Sunday births of their new 'twin sisters'.

Our sisters often related to us of their excitement getting ready for church in their best 'bib & tucker outfits' only to look down and see they forgot to change into their good shoes and had on their 'holy' tennis sneaker shoes!

A bit of information for those of you who perhaps do not know or remember, in our birth year – 1931 – Herbert C. Hoover was the President and Charles Curtis was the Vice President of the USA. Compare the prices of consumer products back then to now. For example, a new Ford auto cost $640.00 and the price of gasoline was ten cents per gallon! A loaf of bread cost eight cents and a pound of butter cost thirty-six cents (but we churned our own butter at our farm – we had a large square glass jug with wooden paddles that my twin and I, as we grew older, took turns churning. A gallon of milk cost fifty cents (we had twenty-seven cows and had our own milk and crème).

Daddy and Mother acquired land near 'Cooper's Corner', located by the road between Auburn and Enumclaw, Washington (State), from our Grandpa Jones. When Daddy built our house it had only two bedrooms so when we were born he added the big bedroom that was built attached to the back of the house over a small creek that flowed through the property. The average cost of a new home in those times was $6,796.00!

Our Mother, Francys Esther (O'Grady) Jones, was 26 years old and Daddy, Robert Elijah Jones, was 38 years old when they married. Mother was a homemaker. She always baked delicious bread and rolls and was a helper for Daddy on the farm. She was an avid reader and had a large book collection that she often loaned out books to the neighbors as there was no library close to our farm. Her lineage was Irish and English. Her father, Francis Walter O'Grady, was Irish and could really dance an 'Irish Jig'. He was a 'horse-trader' by trade. Her Mother, Mignonette Hyde-Howell, was English and the most fantastic cook I ever knew.

Our Father's lineage was Welch and English. His Mother, Rose Alice Emerson, was short in stature (Daddy was only five feet in height) and she was a very happy natured English woman. Grandpa John Wesley Jones was a tall Welshman who always was 'full of yarns' to relate to listeners. Daddy served in World War I, returned home to become a farmer, did machine repair and all sorts of jobs in the farming community. He really was a 'Jack of all trades' and 'master of all'. He even was a 'tree-topper' for hire.

He was known as 'Wildcat Jones', the unbeatable – undefeatable.

III
My Early Recollections
(1930- 1940's)

Being born a twin was quite a novelty in the 'Thirties' as the invention of 'fertility pills' had yet to be invented. Mother always dressed Ilene and me in matching clothes, even to our bed clothing. We resembled each other quite a lot and people seemed interested in us. We always received toys and everything in duplicate and usually we were referred to as *'Twin'* when anyone called us as they weren't always sure who was who! It was fun and we enjoyed playing the 'guessing game'.

In 1934 the Dionne Quintuplets were born in Ontario, Canada. They were the first quintuplets known to have survived infancy. They were identical girls and there was a lot of publicity about them. As the quintuplets grew older, so did we, and we always had colored crayons to use and I remember that the cardboards placed between the cereal-shredded wheat biscuits had printed pictures of the Dionne Quintuplets to color. We would divide the cardboards and color them in matching dresses like we always wore.

We were told that we were 'fraternal twins' –being developed from two different eggs. We were not sure, at that young age, what that was all about and it didn't matter as we grew up like *'two peas in a pod'.*

Our mother often commented that we were easy to care for as we always entertained each other. The folks had two canvas jumper-hanging-seats that were attached to the top of an open door jamb where we faced each other and as we touched hands we could move faster and we would squeal with delight.

As we developed and started forming our personalities it was usually mentioned that I was the *'extrovert'* and Ilene had the *'introvert'* persona.

I was usually the 'practical joker' of the family and enjoyed telling my twin (in later years when I knew about 'such things') that Daddy surely left his *'best sperm'* for the last (me)! I felt my comment funny, but she referred to me as a 'potty mouth'! We weren't always 'double-trouble!'

The summer of 1934 our father purchased a two-wheel cart from Scarff Motors in Auburn, remodeled it and painted the wicker grey with a red base. It was pulled by our Shetland pony we named 'Bluey'. We were in the Auburn Day parade that year so we all felt quite 'special' to partake in the event.

'Bluey' (Shetland pony)-sister-Alice- (in cart- Jack, Ilene, Betty Mignonette, Irene

1933 – Family – Alice, Betty M., Irene, Mother, Daddy, Jack, Ilene

Ilene (L) & Irene (R), 5 Yrs. +/-

Growing up on a farm was a lot of fun for our family. We rode our pony a lot and we always had dogs, cats, chickens and even rabbits as farm pets. In addition we had a large goose that laid large-triple-yolk eggs. Mother used to bake angle-food cakes (before the days of 'box-cakes') and other delicious breads and cinnamon rolls using those large eggs. Our mean gander (male goose) always chased us and 'nipped' at our dresses as we would swirl around on a metal bar that Daddy put up at the woodshed for us. Ilene and I would spend many hours doing various swinging acrobatics.

We had one small cement sidewalk at the front of our house where Ilene and I played 'hop-scotch' a lot marking up the front sidewalk with colored chalk. The moist weather usually brought out 'slugs' – *those slippery-slimy things* – that crawled onto the sidewalk. We learned to sprinkle table salt on them and they would dissolve! Can you imagine? YUK!

Some of our farm chores were to gather the chicken eggs each day and often as we carried them back to the house I would get an 'urge' to pelt my twin in the back with a raw egg! The egg-duel-contest made the output of eggs vary but fortunately, for us, our Mother always blamed the hens!

Our Uncle Charlie and Aunt Mae had the adjoining farm south of our place and we always enjoyed going there with Daddy. They had a large chicken pen with two mean roosters and we were always warned not to go inside the pen. Guess who went inside one day and was attacked by one of the roosters! Ilene ran crying to Uncle Charlie to come to my rescue and he saved me and I wasn't even scolded for my disobedience!

Every summer we had sawed log fire wood dumped near our backyard wood shed. It was our brother's job to stack the wood into piles. He always bribed Ilene and me into helping him stack the wood plus several of his other chores.

Daddy built the first known fireplace in the area. It was in our living room. Ilene and I went with our father to the brick/tile farmer to help choose the colors for the hearth. We thought we must be rich to have such a pretty fireplace where we often sat around it on winter nights listening to the radio programs. We were allowed to stay up late for the programs. We would turn off the lights and get scared as The Inter-sanctum; I Love a Mystery; Jack Armstrong, The All American Boy; Captain Midnight; Lux Theatre and other programs were broadcasted.

IV
Entertainment Before Impact of Technology

The Neuwalkum Creek flowed across part of our property and even under the back part of our house. Our privileges did not include playing in the creek but we often would sneak under the house and walk in the creek when the water wasn't too high even though it was always as cold as ice cubes!

There was a large heavy plank across the creek just alongside the house below our bedroom window. Ilene and I spent many hours making 'mud-pies' and placed them to 'bake' on the plank. We also made our playhouses with rocks and sticks lining the walls, windows, etc. on the dirt areas near the garage and then in the woods located across the highway in the front of our farm. The wooded area was fun because the fir trees kept the space a little dark and provided lots of fir boughs that we used as brooms to sweep the ground and line our make-believe walls. We often carried our 'baked-mud-pies' across the road up to our tree houses. We were not supposed to cross the busy highway so our tree-house playing was unknown to our Mother, or to our Daddy who was always at work.

Having older siblings we often joined them in the various games they did for entertainment. Living seven miles from each of the nearest towns we only went to town on special occasions. After dark the neighbor kids would join us and we'd play 'No Bears out Tonight'. One person would be the 'bear' while the rest of us would hide, then if the 'bear' would catch us before we could run to the home-base we'd be out of the game until all the players were caught. It was a 'scary' but a fun game in the dark.

Another early evening game we often played was 'Anti-I-Over'. We used a tennis ball and divided up into teams (Ilene & I always stayed on the same team). We would toss the ball back and forth over the house.

Ilene and I were about 8/9 years old when Daddy made us wooden stilts and we became so proficient on those that we could run and play catch on them! Simple- yet so much fun – no electronic I-Pads to rob our growing-up fun!

During the summer months we went down to the Green River, located about 1-1/2 miles from our house. The trek to the river usually presented problems for Ilene and me, when we were younger, as the trail downhill to the river was sometimes dark, steep, narrow, slippery, and had a lot of 'devil-club-stinging bushes' that would hurt and cause large red pelts on our skin. We always had our cousins and a neighbor or two join us. The rushing river was quite cold water, being the run-off from the up-streams originating from the foothills of Mt. Rainier. We usually played games like 'Kick or Sit on the Sand Mound' (hiding a 'thistle' or a large 'rock' beneath the mound!). The older kids always had one neighbor boy who they liked, but they referred to him as 'the odd sock', and had him go first then they all laughed! I realize now that was a form of discrimination. The older kids swam in the cold river but we just played at the edges.

The Muckleshoot Indian Tribe had 'fishing rights' and often were down at the river gaffing for steelhead fish – which they sold to some of the local farmers. We were always a little scared of the Indians so kept a lookout for them. They would laugh or shout loud noises just to tease us but never approached us.

All of my siblings, along with our cousins and neighbors, often played in the hay barn a lot and thinking back now it is hard to believe that no one was injured. We had long ropes tied to the center beam and would swing from side-to-side – pretending to be 'Tarzan & Jane'! We also – even more dangerous – burrowed long tunnels into the loose hay and made 'hide-outs' from each other!!! Lucky for us, as we had no cave-ins!!

There was a large cement culvert under the highway where we were not allowed to go but we often did listening to the scary rumble of the vehicles driving overhead. We also tried out our naive skills at smoking cigarettes there! One neighbor girl, our age, stole a pack of Camel cigarettes from Cooper's store and she, Ilene and I hid in the creek and divided up the pack between us to smoke. They enjoyed the process but I did not like it at all so I bit off the ends and would fake a cough so I could spit it out without their knowledge! We always ate raw carrots and radishes, from our garden, in hopes that we would pass the 'smell test' as our Mother's keen sense of smell was sharper than a razor blade!

Another 'smoking event' we did was at our cousins' home in the distant town of Cumberland, Washington. George, Daddy's cousin, and Ollie had an interesting house in the woods that had a long wooden plank driveway and natural, cold mountain water tap on their outside porch. Ilene & I tried out smoking Indian tobacco-weed – using newsprint for paper that burned up in a flame causing our tobacco to fall to the ground! Unknown to us, we singed our eyelashes and brows and really got into trouble when we returned to the house and Mother and Ollie saw us!

Ollie had one of those huge iron hair-permanent machines and Mother had her give Ilene and me our first hair permanent. We were older when that experience happened and it was our first one so we were thrilled to end up with curly hair. It meant no more pigtail braids that Mother did pulling our hair so taunt it make our eyes slant looking oriental –plus hurt us!

If we didn't behave or sassed our Mother she would make us go out and cut the willow branches she would then use to 'switch our bare legs'! I cut larger ones thinking they wouldn't sting as much and perhaps she would be more lenient- NOPE! We played house one time and stuffed pillows into our dresses to create 'breasts' and she made us sit back-to-back so we couldn't face each other or talk then wait for Daddy to come home to punish us! When he saw us he just laughed!

We each had quite a few house and farm chores that needed to be accomplished every day. We would hurry with the chores so we could go to our cousins' place. We treasured our times we were allowed to walk (2miles +/-) over to our closest cousins to play. Uncle Joe (Daddy's widowed brother) had 4 girls and 1 son just like our family. We always enjoyed his homemade root-beer he stored down in the pump-house, and we could help ourselves without permission. We liked the lack of restrictions and freedom to roam at their place!

Our cousins – Uncle Joe's girls – Jo Ann – Ilene – Jeannie – Irene, 1938
(2 smaller children on right?)

Irene – puppy – Ilene

Twins in front of Auburn Grade School
(L) Irene, (R) Ilene

1st Grade Class Group – Front row – #3 Ilene, #4 Irene

V
School Days + Impact Of War

We attended the Auburn Public School system located seven miles south from our farm. The school bus picked us up early and our cousins were picked up two stops later. We all sang the popular songs of the time all the way to and home from school. Our bus driver, as well as the other students, all seemed to enjoy the 'Jones Girls Chorus'.

My twin and I were always dressed alike and the teachers could not tell us apart so they asked our Mother to at least put different colored ribbons on our pigtails as she refused to put different colored dresses on us. During the recesses I convinced Ilene to change out our hair ribbons to confuse the teachers. It worked for a while but then they decided to place us into different rooms so our prank backfired! The separation had a profound affect upon us and then by the second grade my twin failed, due to absences from her illness, and she had to repeat the first grade when I advanced to the second grade. During one of Ilene's absence from school I was so lonely for her I hid under a bush on the playgrounds when another student reported the occasion to the principal – who then came to check on me! I recall her scolding me after I sobbed, *"I have no one to play with"* and her stern response was, *"That is foolish, there are a lot of children out here – STOP crying and get back out on the playground!"* I never liked Mrs. Holt from that day and beyond.

In my third year grade of school I received two small boxes of chocolates one Valentine's Day – one from Kenny M. and one from Francis K.! I certainly thought I must be special but, my love of chocolate candy also made me selfish, and I didn't like having to share the sweets! I finally did share some with my twin.

Our school playground had several bars we were able to swing on and Ilene and I did very well because of the bar at our farm that Daddy put up for us. We both won ribbons at several of the 'bar-swinging contests'. Ilene won the grade school 'Yo-Yo Contest' and I was so proud of her. Guess what she won – yep – another Yo-Yo!

In 1940 my eldest sister, Alice, got married and the following year my twin and I became 'Aunts' for the first time. It was the first to have a baby around our home and we became instant 'babysitters' usually by choice plus it was an opportunity to go to town where our married sister lived.

1939 Family trip to Oregon – Daddy, Jack, Bettey Mignonette, Alice, Mother, (in front – I was in trouble for pushing my knee socks down!) Irene, Ilene

1942 Ilene, Jack, Irene, our 1st nephew – Wayne Parslow at 4 months

1944 – Jack, home on leave from Naval Boot Camp – Daddy, Alice, Mother Betty Mignonette, Irene, Ilene

1944 Brother – Jack Jones – US NAVY

Sister – Betty Mignonette Jones – 2nd Class Spec. X-US NAVY @ WA. D.C. 1945

1947 – Irene age 16, with 1st niece, Marcia Parslow

In 1941, we were ten years old, when World War II was declared. I recall that we had to cover our house windows with heavy dark green blinds so that no lights were visible at night in case the Japanese military would bomb us! War made many changes for us plus it was at this time our Mother had been diagnosed with tuberculosis and had to be put into the Morningside Sanatorium located in the city of Seattle. We were unable to visit her very often and when we did we were always given TB shots that we did not like!

During those war years things were rationed such as sugar and other food items and clothing – especially shoes and 'holy tennis shoes' and going barefoot on the farm was normal and fun! Each household had ration cards issued and stamps that were affixed when items were purchased. Every family had members that volunteered for the military service and our second sister and brother, as well as many of our cousins all went off to serve our country. We were all very proud of them and I am still PRO-military. My three children all served our military.

In the summers of my school years we always picked raspberries at our Uncle Frank's farm to earn money for our school clothing. I always ate a lot of berries so did not fill my boxes as fast as my twin. She usually helped me so we could go to the collection station together. All of our cousins in the area joined us and, like on the school bus, we would sing all the popular songs of the era. Our Uncle Joe decided to raise green string beans and a couple summers we earned our school clothing money picking both beans and berries. Like the berry picking job, I ate my fill of green beans until I got sick so I much preferred the raspberry job.

We had a large Bing sweet cherry tree in our backyard that grew over our porch area. All of my siblings and I enjoyed the fruit and had a hard time picking enough to be canned as we ate more than we picked! One summer our Mother told Ilene and I not to climb up into the tree as the berries had worms in them. We, of course, did not obey and snuck up the tree many times until one day we took time to check out the flesh of the fruit only to find many small white *'wiggly'* worms in every cherry. *"You grow up the day you have the first real laugh at yourself"*, as Ethel Barrymore once said.

I had no fear of climbing trees and would often climb our pear tree higher than Ilene would climb. I would tell her I was preparing to 'flap my wings and fly away'!

Her tears begging me to stay and come down from the tree always worked.

1943 – New permanents – 1st ever of non-matching skirts (13 yrs. Old) Irene and Ilene

1941 – Only professional photo taken @ Melin Studio – WA.
Alice, Jace, B. Mignonette, Irene, Ilene
(The photographer had Jack and Ilene stand on boxes for height.)

Our House

Our Farm

Daddy and Mother

VI
Farm Life – Sex Education – Puberty

The first five chapters of this memoir describe a lot of my early formative years; however, I feel the need to express some of my likes/dislikes and then my puberty years that all contribute to the person I am as of this 2016 writing.

Living on a farm was one of many blessings I have enjoyed in my life plus having my twin always by my side. Our eldest sister left the farm to marry and then the two next siblings went off to serve our country leaving our parents and us on the farm. Mother had been in and out of hospitals, due to her TB and then her back problems, so Ilene and I did most of the housework/cooking and helping Daddy when we could. Mother had to wear a back brace and spent a lot of time sitting in her rocker, reading and chewing Dentyne gum – which she would not let us have and every time she made a 'popping' noise I would resent it and her more!

Mother did a lot of reading and had many books that she would loan out to neighbors. I recall having to dust them and make sure they were arranged properly on the shelves. I sometimes resented the work, thinking I could be in town and do the fun things my other classmates were able to enjoy. I now realize looking back to those times how selfish I was in resenting Mother and her books (but not the gum). I loved her but did not always like her as I felt she was too strict at discipline!

I never cared to read her books – but did read the fly-leaf on the covers and would use that info to cheat on making book reports that were due at school. I remember one book, 'Forever Amber', that she acquired and we were told we were not allowed to read that book! I, of course, choose to read that book at night after everyone was in bed. I'm sure that it would be compared to almost being scriptural with a lot of the literature/movies/TV and any social media that is available today!

Our Mother was quite reserved on any form of 'sex-education' and even when our rooster was mating with the hens – she would only say, "*Oh they are fighting again!*" Then on another occasion in our back pasture when the bull mounted one of the female heifers Mother said, "*Oh, they are just playing leap frog again!*" Once Daddy and a friend tried to mate our 'Bluey' (Shetland pony) to a large mare when Mother made Ilene and I go to our bedroom – she pulled down the heavy dark green window shades – and told us not to look outside and just to play in our room! We, of course, peeked around the shades to observe the barn activity but had no clue as to what or why such an activity was going on!

Mother had our older sister take us to the movie in town that was describing the results of sex and communicable diseases. I remember how shocking it was. Some girls even fainted during the ordeal! It was at this time (1945 – we were 14 years old) when I was put in a Catholic hospital because of my left clavicle infection operation and Mother and Ilene came to see me. Ilene started her menstrual period and didn't know what was wrong! A Nun at the hospital helped my twin with the necessary steps then brought her to Mother who then promptly said goodbye to me and took Ilene to our older sister's place to have Alice explain the facts of life. We both were still quite naïve! No television or other social media to educate us in those times.

We had to do the family laundry every Saturday in addition to the normal house work. We had an old metal Maytag wringer washing machine and two large rinse tubs (one for clear water and the second one had bluing rinse water). We had five long, approximately twenty feet, clotheslines in the back yard. Mother always insisted that we hang all the clothes in proper order – the sheets and towels on the outside lines to hide the underwear items on the inner lines. We also ALWAYS had to hang Ilene's and my dresses that matched side by side!

We tried to rush with the laundry and then the weekly scrubbing, dusting, washing those darn wood kitchen cabinets –(in reflecting back now – makes me wonder why the paint didn't wear off–?) then do all the other chores so we could receive permission to go over to our closest cousins' place to play.

The task ahead of us is never as great as the Power behind us.

About this time – in my growing-up years – I must admit to one of my 'rebellious streaks' – (remember, I am the *extrovert twin'*). One day I slammed the kitchen door and had to re-open and close it *'gently'* five times as punishment. On the fifth closing I slammed it again with enough force the large kitchen window broke!!! I then had to hoe five long rows of field corn for that punishment!! Of course, my twin came to my aid and helped me get the job done.

One summer, when we were older, I decided that we should cut our hair short and convinced my twin that she would go first! I actually tied her wrists and ankles to the kitchen wooden chair then had her sip some beer with a straw convincing her it would relax her! The end result was our necessary trip to town to buy Toni home permanents we gave each other. That resulted in our family/friends giving us the name of 'Bubble Heads'!

During our middle-school years (grades 7-9) we attended the Jr. High School located at a different end of town. Finally by the 7th grade puberty had greeted me with my menstrual cycle but we both still had flat chests compared to our female classmates! I felt so UN-feminine that I would take a Kotex sanitary pad and cut it in two then place it into my empty bra to create some form. I was the only one in my class with 'square' shape boobs! I forgot to trim the corners. Our Home-Economics teacher was also 'flat-chest', but she could afford the *rubber falsies*. Many times one breast was high and the other quite low which caused me to giggle and send notes to my classmates about the fact and, of course, I got into trouble for that!

My lack of physical maturity did not curb my interest in the opposite sex and I had a knack for flirting. My motto was, 'Don't wait for the ship to come in – row out to meet it! ' I joined all the clubs and became involved in many extra circular activities although having to ride the school bus home every afternoon did curb a lot of participation at times. If I happened to miss the bus ride my twin would cover for me and then give me heck when I managed to get a ride home later!

The love of my life for the three years of Jr. High School was the best boyfriend I had during all my school years. I shall call him 'Larry'. He never took advantage of our relationship other than a kiss, holding hands and some hugs. We used to write long love letters on the standard lined notebook paper. Larry used to fold his 'missives of endearments' into tiny squares – about the size of a fifty-cent coin! I was never able to re-fold them so filed them away into a box I hid in our bedroom so my twin – or worse yet— my Mother might find them! He was a good 'kisser'! Seventy years later I wish I had kept one of those 'love notes' to read today. It would no doubt be humorous, entertaining but certainly not be filed under 'erotic', IF my memory is correct?

Larry went to San Francisco, California on a trip with his parents and upon his return he gave me a small gift. It was a tiny metal figurine of a fisherman in a yellow slicker coat and hat with a fishing pole, line and little fish attached. Crazy as it may seem, I do have the 'little fisherman figurine' still today – 70+/ – years later!

Larry and family moved to another town and I started my Senior High School years – new boyfriends, experiences and sex education on the fast tract!

1946 – Ilene, Irene (I stood on grass so our shoulders were even. I don't think those were 'real boobs!'

1947 – Twins @ 16 yrs. – Ilene – Irene

The last three school years really flew by for my twin and me, as by this time our Mother had left our Dad so we grew up quite fast – not physically – but worldly, *we thought*? Daddy had taught us how to drive a car, change a tire, oil, and he always helped us with our school homework, etc. He never knew that we took the car and drove around through the country cemetery seeing how fast we could make the turns without upending the stone grave markers!! I used to miss catching the school bus so I could drive the car to school and convince Ilene it would be OK! We also took gasoline from the farm pump, without permission, and learned how to turn back the gallon-output lever!! If Daddy knew, he never told us.

He also taught us how to weld, and do work in his machine shop where he repaired things, built machinery/wagons, etc. and helped his brothers and neighbors. He milked the cows morning and night plus continued his day job at the shipyards in Seattle. He was lenient with us for dating boys but we did have a curfew hour to return home! We now had full run of the household, cooking, chores, etc.

I was sixteen in the sophomore year and thought I was 'hot stuff'! One of my dates, that came to pick me up for a dance, was a very tall, thin boy named Charles XXXXX. I remember that I was so flustered when introducing him to Daddy that I said, *"Daddy, I'd like you to meet Charles Atlas!"* My Daddy's response was, *"Well damn son, looks like you forgot to eat your Wheaties!"* Charles just laughed.

I managed to get a date with one of the most desired (by the female students) senior fellows from the basketball team. It was a double date and we went to a drive-in movie using his father's car. The other couple became quite promiscuous in the back seat when my date suggested we walk to the popcorn hut to get some pop.

I was smart enough to know what was going on and truly embarrassed. When we returned to the car and the movie ended so we drove to an overlook to park and 'spoon' when the 'hot-couple' were at it again in the back seat! Lucky for me we just kissed but when we were ready to leave the car had a flat tire and no spare! My date and I walked to the nearest place we could to find a phone to call his parents for help. They lived across the street from my eldest sister where I was spending the night.

My sister told me that I was not to date him ever again after I explained what had happened that night. I was further embarrassed from that date by finding out at school that both fellows bragged to their basketball team about their 'manly achievements!' I was unfoundedly labeled as a 'loose date' and **never** dated him again! I was hurt and crushed. It was a real introduction of 'sex education'.

"Nor hell a fury like a woman scorned!" quoted from playwright William Congreve. I made it a point to justify my action and discredit his bragging!

My junior year in high school proved to be one of a lot of fun, some learning, out of credit demands, and lots of social activities. I was chosen the Junior Princess for the Homecoming festivities and wore my pretty new blue formal complete with the rhinestone tiara! A first for me, plus I was the secretary-treasurer for our class and had a lead part in the school play that year. I joined all the various club activities including the Ski Club and learned how to snow ski. The only money I had to spend was from babysitting and it was rather sparse. We were not given allowance, as some of our classmates had, so ski lift tickets were hard to obtain!

I wasn't able to go very often but enjoyed the thrill of 'FLYING' down the slopes.

I didn't know then that I would have the opportunity to 'FLY' the slopes of France, Austria and Germany in my future.

Irene – 1949

VII
Marriage — Childbirth — Etc.
1950

Fantasies feed our souls and as I entered my final year of high school education I had my 'flying desire' fueled into thinking I could become an airline stewardess. I could just envision me in the 'snappy' airline attire and getting to *'FLY'* off to many different places in the world! I was simply sure that my 'five foot two, twinkling eyes of blue' would have me airborne and was I crushed when I found out I was not tall enough!

I had a bout with skin eczema and was given the 'blue-light' treatments to clear my skin. I had a few facial pimples at the time – no doubt from puberty reasons – and the nurse decided that I should also have the light on my face. She left the room, as was customary, but forgot to return at the allowed time and the result was severe skin burns on both my face and hands. (Today the medical facility would have been sued!). The bad result for me was that I was unable to do the shorthand and typing exams for my senior credits and would be unable to graduate with my class. My class advisors were of no help and graduation was only a few months away. At the time I was currently dating my boyfriend from the next town who wanted to marry me!

I thought marriage held excitement and fun and had lost my virginity by then so felt it was the right move for me. I was barely eighteen years of age so I said *"YES"* to the future father of my children. His parents were NOT in approval of any marriage. They wanted their son to go to college and made it quite clear that I was just a farmer's daughter, not graduated nor of the 'social status' of their family! My husband-to-be told them that I was 'pregnant' and we had to get married! He did NOT tell me of his comment to the folks. He only told me his parents said I should first go, with his older sister who would take me to their doctor, to be examined for a 'diaphragm' which was required for all brides-to-be. Also, his parents would pay the doctor. I assumed that was protocol so I obeyed. They only wanted to find out if I was pregnant and then to be fitted for the contraption they gave me to make sure I would not get pregnant! Even though I wasn't a virgin by now, nor pregnant, I was still rather naive!

My future in-laws were considered influential in the local town, financially well established and definitely domineering concerning all of their children! My husband, Carl LaVan Johansen, was nineteen days younger than I was. We were both eighteen when we married. The second night of our honeymoon my monthly period started and I had to ask my 'Hubby' to go buy some kotex for me! He returned to the motel with the item plus a six-pack of beer saying, *"I might as well get drunk!"* which he did! Our first night returning home we spent at the in-laws home sleeping in his former bedroom. His brother, Wayne, five years-older, unknown to us had fixed the wooden slats that held the box springs under the bed. It collapsed with a loud 'thud' that night! The close brothers played many practical jokes on each other and me. We three had a great relationship.

Nine months and eleven days later I gave birth to my first born child, my son, Daniel LaVan, who weighed in at 9lbs. 10-1/2oz.!!! What an experience I had after twenty-four hours of hard labor to deliver such a large baby. From barely having 'boobs' in high school to marriage-pregnancy-then nursing I became quite 'top-heavy' much to both my husband's and son's delight!

Being a wife and birthing children was to become my main occupation for the next four years! While nursing my son I had no menstrual periods so was unaware that I had become pregnant again in 1951 when I had a miscarriage at three months. In 1952 I was pregnant once more and had a baby girl who was born premature and died three days after birth.

At this time of my life the doctor advised me that my husband and I had the RH-Factor blood problem and should not get pregnant again. It was too late – as I was already pregnant for the fourth time! I gave birth to my second son, Lee who was born on his paternal grandmother's birthday, December 7th, much to her and my delight. It was fortunate that he did not need a blood transfusion as the medical people said would be necessary. Darwin Lee weighed 8 lbs. 4 oz. He was smaller in size at birth, after my first son, so I was worried but needlessly as he became a little robust trooper, hard to keep still at times, but lots of fun watching him grow and interact with his brother.

1954 I had been married four years, pregnant four times and again advised by my doctor that I should not have any more babies and have my tubes tied for that reason. It was too late, as once again, I was pregnant! Believe me; I did do many other things than 'pro-create' as with two small children to care for and lots of homemaking chores I also had to pick up the slack for my sometimes errant husband.

We lived next to my in-laws farm and I usually had to keep a lookout for them walking across the field to see their grandchildren so I could hide the beer bottles and cigarette butts that their son created! The folks were nice, but rather strict on such behavior.

At the end of my fourth married year, and my fifth pregnancy, I gave birth to my second daughter, Diane Laurene, who was delivered via cesarean section and I then had my fallopian tubes tied to prevent any further pregnancies.

I believe, as with most Mothers, having babies and raising them is one of the most fulfilling and rewarding experiences for any woman. I referred to my children as my 'Three D's' as we named them. They were/are my triple pride and joy.

Irene & LaVan Johansen – 2-15-1950

1953 Enumclaw, WA. – sons, Darwin Lee – 3 mo. + Dan – 3 yrs.

1954- Dan 4 years, Me, Diane 6 month

My 3D's Sunday school graduation.

1957- Our second farm @ Outlook, WA.

1958 – 3rd farm – Quincy, WA – my '3' D's
Dan – 6yrs., Darwin – 3 yrs, Diane – 2 yrs.

My in-laws required that we baptize and raise our children in their Lutheran denomination which we did. I made sure my children attended Sunday school and church throughout their upbringing but their father never went back to church once he left his parents' control.

The fifth year of our marriage we moved to the eastern part of Washington State to farm. That move was mainly to avoid the close observations of my in-laws plus my husband's choice to distance himself from them and his eldest brother.

Our first farm was twelve acres of asparagus that we cut by hand every morning at the unthinkable hour of four in the morning. It was necessary to have the vegetables into the market very early in the morning. It was a back-breaking job and then I would fix breakfast for my children, husband and next help him at our large feedlot with the grain/hay output, fence repair-etc. I did enjoy the farm life style.

Our next farming adventure was buying 120 acres at the location of Outlook, Washington. We built another large feedlot for the cattle we raised for the in-laws' meat market. We also raised alfalfa, field corn, and sugar beets. We had a Holstein dairy cow that I milked every morning and evening. I remember giving her leftover watermelon pieces that turned her milk pink and my children refusing to drink it! It did have an unusual flavor as I recall.

During this period of my marriage I began to realize the absence of my husbands' hay hauling venture and his drinking was causing a strain on our marriage. I really prayed for marital guidance from my church.

We moved again to our third farming experience to Quincy, Washington, an area where we purchased another 120 acres with a nicer farmhouse. Again, we built a large feedlot to care for the cattle purchased by the in-laws for their meat market. The dry land was undeveloped so we planted alfalfa. We purchased a hand-pipe irrigation system that had to be moved every morning and evening. My husband was still hauling hay back and forth over the mountains, added to his drinking and many absences that required me to pick up the slack of his job on the farm. I now had the help of my eldest son each early morning before getting the three children ready for school. The two younger children tagged along as we moved the water pipes each evening, along with the other feed lot chores. It was becoming apparent to me at this time that I should no longer continue to stay married to LaVan. I knew I had to find myself a job to be able to care for my children and myself.

I applied for a legal secretary position in town but had to pass a typing test given at the next town twenty miles distance. On my rush to the testing site I was caught speeding. The officer said I was going 103 miles per-hour! I didn't know the car went that fast and was told I had to report to the local judge in my town. That was quite an experience as the Judge 'hit' on me and said he would reduce my speeding fine IF I would come upstairs and see his 'etchings'! I paid the fine, told the Judge to *"Go to hell"* and happily I ended up getting the job at the law office.

I told my husband that I wanted a divorce and he just laughed then got drunk with one of the gals he was seeing at the time. My divorce simply unglued my in-laws (the first in their family) and I paid dearly for that. His parents and older brother then made my departure as difficult as they could and, of course, placed all the blame upon me. They did what I would determine a 'snow job' at my children and my expense of manipulating all the assets so I was left barely existing on my new legal secretary salary. I was just happy to move on and wanting the best for my children and myself.

I soon found that being a 'divorcee' was not easy – as most of my married friends looked upon me as a threat to their marriage! I started dating our real estate agent, who was also divorced, and became sexually involved with him. Being a good mother and a good lover and juggling my former husbands' exploitations that were also going on in front of me and my children's' eyes in the small town was difficult to say the least! I still was determined to stay single for at least three years.

1963 – Irene, Alice, Jack, Mignonette, Ilene (siblings)

Daniel LaVan – Diane Laurene – Darwin Lee

VIII
Second Marriage - Foreign Living
1960's

The three year pact I made with myself only lasted two years! Again trying to be (what I thought) was a good mother and still seeing and having sex with my soon to be 'husband number two' required a lot of finesse so only lasted a little over two years!

John H. Butler, husband number two, had a real estate firm and also did farming in the area. John's faith was also Lutheran so we continued at our church. He took me to the Hawaiian Islands on our honeymoon. It was a first experience there for me and my twin sister and brother-in-law took care of my three D's for me. I continued my legal secretary position, cared for my children and helped John with the real estate business. We, including my three D's, planted 120 acres of dwarf yellow delicious apple trees which was a new crop experience.

In 1965 we moved to México City. John received an opportunity, via one of his brothers, to present and promote to President Diaz Ordiaz a plan to build a deep sea port on the west coast of México. John had been in the US Air Force/Pilot, real estate development and had an engineer's degree. He and his brother had done extensive investigation into the feasibility of such an undertaking. The port was to be located at Topolabampo which has ample water depth to service large sea-going vessels. (It is my understanding as of today that the port may become a reality!) The only other deep sea port for México at that time was/is at Merida.

The three year adventure – and it was an adventure for all of us – ended up uncompleted due to the many stalling and 'graft' situations by the political parties involved. We had no financial backing for our part in the proposal and also my husband's lineage, mainly Norwegian, did not accept the 'manna' custom! Plus, we were using our own funds and could not afford to continue the many bribes and gratuities expected as was their culture.

The entertaining of some persons of the highest held positions of the country and other dignitaries certainly was a new experience for me. I had a full-time maid, who was an excellent cook and friend, who assisted me in the many dinners and soirees that we held at our penthouse. Both John and I felt the gifts, plus booze and flowers, expected by our many guests, were 'overboard' to our way of thinking.

His secretary, a shapely, long legs, eyelashes, hair style and 'big breasts', was fluent in English and Spanish and at his side most of every meeting. Her mother and sometimes my maid were my caretakers for my children who were always 'shuffled off' whenever we entertained. The 'officials' always had private – gun toting – bodyguards stationed outside our private elevator! It was quite an experience!

During our extended three year sojourn in Mexico, John had asked me if I would consider having a child with him. He convinced me that his mother had his youngest sibling when his mother was forty years of age. Because I was only thirty-four years – perhaps I could have my fallopian tubes UN-tied and try for a baby! I thought hopefully it would bring my three D's and John into a tighter knit family.

I had the US Embassy's medic, Dr. Guzman, perform the surgery and before long I did, in fact, become pregnant. However, I had another miscarriage and, even though our sexual compatibility was great, I did not conceive after that time.

The foreign living experience was an opportunity for my children and me to learn the Spanish language as well as their customs. John took the Spanish speaking classes with me but was not as fluent as I became because he had his secretary to translate for him every day. My eldest son, who was fifteen years of age at the time we arrived, was required to study/know two foreign languages other than his native tongue so he studied French at the French Institute in the evenings. My younger son and daughter attended a private parochial school that only spoke Spanish and they became fluent in the language quite fast.

My husband was, of course, disappointed and even bitter of the failed venture. I felt the experience for myself and my children outweighed the absence of our family and friends over the three years living in Mexico.

We had the opportunity and cultural exposure a lot of people never have.

Irene, John Butler & Irene's children lived in Mexico City 1965-66-67

1966- MEXICO CITY

Dan, Diane, Darwin – Mexico City, 1966

Irene – Mexico City -1966

1968-1969

Three years later we returned to the USA and settled at Santa Clara, California. John tried a new position of selling life insurance. My children were now enrolled into schools and I, also, went back to school to obtain that 'long-ago missed High School diploma!' I then continued taking many college courses to fulfill my long desire to learn & paint fine art.

I want to share one such class I took at the Foothills College in Palo Alto. I was thirty-seven at the time and thought I was quite 'worldly' with my previous experiences and travels. I enrolled in a 'human-body' watercolor drawing class and began to make friends with an over-weight 'hippie', who was dressed in an ugly purple smock, and wasn't talking with anyone else. The professor, a young male, entered the room, clapped his hands and my 'fat friend' dropped her purple smock and clumsily plopped her fat, naked body atop a large table in the center of the room! I was flabbergasted as I was positioned such that I looked at her derriere and the two balloon boobs dangling close to the edge of the table!

He advised us to use only two colors of paint and by the time he approached my station I was still in shock and had a blank paper on my easel. He made a smart remark to me so I quickly splashed two blue circles and a splotch of purple for nipples and her anus – which was all I could see! He laughed, slapped me on the shoulder and said, *"I think we'll get along great!"* It was my first of many classes in various schools of higher learning ala *'California style!'*

John was becoming stricter in his discipline with my children which caused some conflict for the whole family. One example was that my second son, Darwin Lee, was given a reading assignment in school to read and report on the book 'To Sir with Love'. Darwin wasn't too keen on reading it, as I recall, and tossed the book onto the couch. John picked the book up, read a few pages, and was outraged that Darwin had chosen to report on that novel! He made a real issue of Darwin's choice of reading material even though he explained it was his assignment – not his choice. I went to the school to check out Darwin's assignment and found out he was telling the truth. I tried to explain it to John and only received a stern response of, *"Oh, that's right – you always take your children's side!"*

During this time of our California living, Darwin Lee called his father and chose to go live with him. He told me he'd run away if I didn't agree to his leaving. As a Mother, it tore my heart strings to the breaking point. He did not get along with John, and his father was quite the opposite and promised him all the 'fun things' he could do. Rather than all the turmoil in the household I relented, let my 15 year old son go, and regretted his choice to this date.

Even though John was a good provider for us, his strict ways were becoming to stress the family. My eldest son, Daniel, had learned to play the accordion when I first married John and then Dan didn't play it during our Mexico living but became interested in playing the electric organ John had. Dan played quite well and at the time the Beatles music was popular. Dan purchased the song, 'Hey Jude' and was playing it when John had another one of his 'parental unreasonable outbursts' and forbade Dan to play or have any of the Beatles' music in our house! Guess what, some years later (after Dan had joined the Air Force) John started playing and liked the music of 'Hey Jude!'

At this time I chose to go back on birth control pills because I realized that I did not want to become pregnant with a child by John.

Irene's graduation – 1969

Di, Dar, Dan – CA., 1969

Colorado Springs, CO. – my sons – 1971

1971 – Son Darwin Lee joins US ARMY

Daniel L. Johansen, 1971-1975 Airman 1st class – USAF

Daughter – Diane joins US Army – 1974
Spec 4 – goes to Germany

1969-70 +

After two years of living in California we moved to Colorado Springs, Colorado. John went into the business of real estate sales. He became 'obsessed' with his drive to recoup the money we lost with the Mexican venture and he was now determined to become a 'millionaire!'

At this time my eldest son, Dan, joined the US Air Force 1971, so he was absent from the home and my daughter had just entered High School. I almost had an 'empty nest syndrome' feeling. There was nothing that John wouldn't give to me except his time for us to do things together. We still enjoyed a very satisfactory sexual life but beyond the bed-sheets I often led a single lifestyle!

I chose to go back to work and was hired as the top legal secretary for the head officer of a large national bank in our town. A few years later John and I had separated and then reunited a couple of times during this period of my life. I went to our church and also a marriage counselor for advice and help. It was difficult for me to accept another failed marriage, by my choice, but I wanted more out of life than rings and roses! I simply wanted to FLY AWAY!

My extra curricular activities were mostly with my daughter and her friends on the ski slopes and even taking scuba diving lessons. The scuba lessons resulted in my long encounter with my *French Connection* explained in my next chapter of this memoir and in my book 'THE SIX MONTHS *PROPOSAL*' published in 2014.

1972 +++

My illicit affair, with my 'French connection,' left me with a HUGE guilt complex and severe abdominal pain. I did not know what was causing my pain, other than self imposed stress, when I collapsed on our street a couple nights after I had, once again, returned to John to try to repair our marital differences. I ended up in one of the local hospitals where the medical staff could not find the reason for my severe condition! I was pronounced 'dead' and as one of the interns was removing the last tubes from me he discovered a faint pulse and everything after that was one fast 'blur' for me! The Lord had more plans for me.

My serious medical condition turned out to be a tubal pregnancy! Was it from John or Roland (the Frenchman)? When I separated from John the first time I quit taking birth control pills out of vanity as they created a skin discoloration on my forehead! To quote William Shakespeare, "*Lord, what fools these mortals be*!"

After I returned home from my hospital stay John suggested that I fly to my twin sister's home to recuperate, so I did. He never phoned me to inquire as to how I was feeling but the 'Frenchman' not only called several times but he even sent me some roses! I then had to confess to my twin of my extra-marital affair!

She wasn't overly fond of John but she sure did raise her eyebrows and shook her head at me about my 'French connection'!

"The things our friends (or relatives) do with us and for us form a portion of our lives, they strengthen our personalities." quoted from Goethe.

1972 – Colorado Springs – our 1st meeting

IX
'Third Times a Charm'
Foreign Travels – Art – Writing

I moved out of our home and filed for a divorce before John could or possibly would talk me into reuniting with him again. I also then quit my job at the bank and made all the necessary plans to FLY AWAY to Europe with Roland Joseph Coatta, my guide –the *'French Frog'* (my pet name for him along with 'RJ').

Roland had filed for his divorce before I had. He had just retired, after twenty-one years of active service, from the United States Air Force. He was then working at a civilian job and agreed to quit his job and travel to Europe with me for my six months planned itinerary. At first he was rather reluctant to travel with me, not having the funds to contribute for the extensive excursion, but he said, *'OK'* after I told him, *"I'm going with or without you, so make up your mind!"*

"The journey of a thousand miles begins with one step", Loc-tse

The following six months (*My 'Fly Away' Experience*) – which turned into three years – were, without a doubt, the most exciting, sexy, rewarding, interesting years of my life to date.

I could relate a lot about those glorious years but it would be redundant for me, so I suggest that you read my book, *The Six Months Proposal'* published in 2014. *(Based On Real Life! – But Written As Fiction)*.

During those 'six-months', that really turned into three years, I was fortunate enough to enroll in the Herzfeld Art School in Wiesbaden, Germany. I wanted to learn the 'Old Master Technique' of oil painting and I did learn that plus many more mediums and techniques. I achieved my diploma that qualified me as an art instructor. Being so interested in art it was a bonus for me as I was able to visit the many famous art museums in Europe as we toured twenty-six countries.

I continued to study every chance I had about art and painting. I also kept a daily dairy about my experiences which I used to write my Six Months Proposal novel.

1974 – Wales

1975 Germany

1974 – Irene @ Plankstdat, Germany

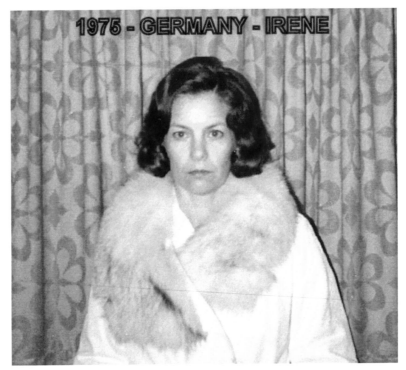

1975 Germany

1974- FRANCE

Irene – Belgium

1974- VAL THORENS, FRANCE

1975- AUSTRIA with IRENE

1974- VAL THORENS - FRANCE

1974 – Tivoli, Italy

Roland & Irene

Paris, France

1976 marriage @ San Antonio, TX

1976- FLAGSTAFF

1987

Flagstaff Arizona

1976-1991 – Flagstaff, AZ

1977- IRENE -FLAGSTAFF, AZ.

1978- IRENE- FLAGSTAFF, AZ.

1976
BACK IN THE USA

Our family and friends know that Roland and I married in San Antonio, Texas in 1976 as we were returning to our former Colorado area. I chose the date – November 19th – (my father's birth-date) I joked with RJ my reason being I was married so many times that the date would help me remember our 'special date'!

By now I wanted to marry him, even though I refused the six months of proposals that resulted into three years (do read my book – The Six Months Proposal – it is special and tells of the 'fun' – three years we enjoyed abroad.) The other reason for my saying 'yes' was we had to face our families who had nearly disowned us!

Arriving Colorado Springs we were somewhat disillusioned by the traffic, the 'hippies' and other changes that were not there prior to our going to Europe. We chose to travel to Mazatlan, Mexico to bask in the sun and decide where we should settle and what employment we should seek.

Along the way we stopped at Flagstaff, Arizona and felt it had all the attractions – four seasons, snow skiing, University, theatre, fewer cars and people – so we ended up there. RJ went to work selling real estate, and I worked at the University in the law department. We purchased our first home that had a small art studio and large garden in the back yard.

I continued my desires for creating art and took many new courses in a variety of art classes whenever possible. We snow skied every winter – (and yes, we even made love in our back yard snow drifts!)– We did cross country and down-hill skiing with our friends and always went to all the dances in the area. Life was lots of fun for us. Our marriage was what I would wish for every couple to experience in their lifetime.

I left my legal secretary job at the University and took the real estate exam and then joined Roland in real estate sales. We later joined the Century 21 firm and became the top sales agents for that firm for several years. After some time the stress of our profession and the 7,000+ elevation was the cause, according to our doctor, for RJ's first heart attack. The doctor suggested that he find another source of employment and move to a lower elevation.

We still had the wanderlust to travel in our desires so we purchased a 28ft. travel trailer, traded our auto for a van to pull the 'house of wheels', and decided to give a one year try at early retirement. We rented our new home we had recently built in the country club, much to my uncertainty, but I didn't want my sweetheart to have another heart attack! I, again, kept a daily notebook and wrote a short story I titled 'Over the Hill and Picking up Speed' about our trailer/travels. We had many fun (don't come knocking, when our trailer's a rocking) but also some real 'hair-raising' experiences during our road travels.

After our first year 'on the road' we returned to Flagstaff to check on our house when the renters requested a year extension. The rent was making our mortgage payments and we had become used to the freedom and travel experiences so we did re-rent our beautiful home. I managed to do my art projects, writing and enjoy the trailer lifestyle. So much so we ended up six years on the road!

At the end of our second year of RV-travels Roland inquired from a minister, where we attended a church service, what were the steps necessary for the opportunity to join the Peace Corps. After Roland professed his desire to serve the Lord then the minister asked me how I felt about going into the ministry field. I replied, *"Well Pastor, I read about some ladies in the Peace Corps serving in Africa and being raped and then murdered! I wouldn't mind the rape part, but I sure didn't want to be sent home in a pine box!"* The Pastor stood up and said, *"I don't think you folks are quite ready to serve the Lord."* Roland didn't get mad at me and then laughed saying, *"I guess he didn't appreciate your sense of humor, sweetheart."*

CHRISTAIN MINISTERY

It was 1989 when we encountered RV travelers at a state campground who introduced and invited us to join their ministry group called SOWERS. The group volunteered to help where needed throughout the USA and México. It is like the group called Habitat for Humanity that former President Jimmy & Roslyn Carter are serving. In fact, we did do a ministry project with them at Tijuana, México a year later.

We were accepted into the SOWERS organization and our first three-month project was at an orphanage, Hogar Para Niño's, located at Colonia Vicinte Guerrero, located approximately three-hundred (+/-) miles south of the California/Tijuana/ México border down the Baja peninsula. It was a moving experience and after our time there I wrote a short story of our experiences I titled 'Baja Babies'.

We continued to serve with the SOWERS Christian ministry projects at many different locations in the USA and again in México the full year of 1989. That experience led us to join the organization of YWAM where we attended a bible college in Los Angeles, California for five months. Our YWAM group then traveled to Europe where we performed Christian mimes in Germany (3 cities); Poland (38 cities); France (3 cities) and Switzerland (5 cities). It was another rewarding experience for both of us.

"Good actions are the invisible hinges on the doors of heaven", Victor Hugo

-SOWERS Ministry- Jan./Feb./Mar. 1989
1st project – Orphanage @ Baja, Mexico (Taught school – wrote book, Baja Babies)

3rd project – Sept & Oct 1989 – Mt. Lake Ranch & Chapel project, Dandridge, TN (painted signs)

Discipleship Training School
Certificate of Completion

THIS TO CERTIFY THAT

IRENE COATTA

has successfully met the Spiritual, Academic and Practical standards as set forth by

The Board of Regents

of

University of the Nations
Youth With A Mission

Given at Los Angeles, California on this ___12TH___ day of ___MAY___, 1990

School Director   Assistant Director

1989 – Bible College @ YWAM, California

Brandenburg Square, Germany
Performing 'King of Hearts Mimes'

4-18-1990 @ Berlin Wall, Germany
(+3 cities)

France – (+3 cities) Pompadou Square

La Gault La Foret, France
200 yr. old Chapel – cleaning

Gryfolwa, Poland (total of 38 cities)

Jelina Gora, Poland

Irene's 'silver-fox fur hat' – Krakow, Poland

YWAM's Castle @ Hurlach, West Germany

Austria – performing Mimes

Switzerland (5 cities)

YWAM Base @
Eingen-Thunersee, Switzerland

YWAM Base @ Lausaune, Switzerland
(pulled weeds & washed windows)

After three years of ministry I convinced RJ we should move back into our home in Flagstaff. We did and within three months he experienced another heart issue so we immediately put our home on the market and sold it. Our fifteen years in the high country was over so we moved to the Arizona desert (lower elevation) settling at Sun Bird Golf Resort, a retirement community, in Chandler, Arizona.

X

The Consummate Artist

I was advised by several family members, plus a few friends, who have read my memoirs that I should put a chapter about my various accomplishments in the field of fine art. I chose this chapter title from an article (enclosed-photo #88) written by Bob Neuman of the Sun Bird News-August 2015 issue – that covers some of my artistic endeavors.

I also am attaching a selected few photos of some paintings and murals accomplished to-date (2015).

June 29, 2015- installed the Sun Bird Library art project
'S-B Library Bookshelf'- 15" high x 70"wide-acrylic
Painted on foam-core - 85 books+ cat+ gecko + (1) bookend

75 TILE MURAL CUSTOM DESIGNED AND HAND PAINTED MURAL
CHINA PAINT-KILN FIRED: ARTIST-IRENE JONES COATTA - 1984

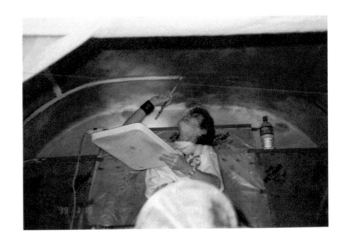

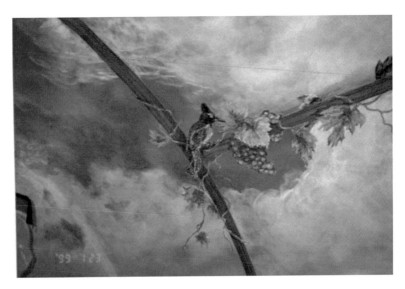

7' high-37'wide-MURAL
@ INSTITUTO CURTURAL
DE OCCIDENTE, A.C.
MAZATLAN, MEXICO-
IRENE JONES COATTA,
ARTIST – 2000-2001

3 weeks 2000- six 10 hr. days
3 weeks 2001- six 10 hr. days
120 hrs total - no chg.
gift to School

I JC STUDIO
Irene Jones Coatta
1542 East Doral Drive
Chandler, Arizona 85249-4074

IJC Studio
1542 E. Doral Dr.
Chandler, AZ 85249-4047
Phn. 480-896-8437
Email: coatta@netzero.net
www.IJCstudio.com

Religious Mural donated 2005 22-10thrs days

30'H x 27'W

14 portraits - acrylic capilla de San Francisco Xavier Puesta del Sol - Mazatlán México 2005

I JC STUDIO
Irene Jones Coatta
1542 East Doral Drive
Chandler, Arizona 85249-4074

St. Joseph Catholic Church- Harlowton, Montana – 2007 –
glass painted 12 windows- 40"x76.5" + 2 windows 2'5"x5'

2007

Sun Bird Golf Resort – 2014 exterior patio mural – 6ft. x 5ft. arc

Three Doves– San Xavier
Oil 48x60

Sea Shells
Mixed Media 20x24

Irene Jones Coatta

IJC Studio
Home: 480-895-6437
Cell: 480-720-7469
1542 E. Doral Dr.
Chandler, AZ 85249-4074
Email: ricoatta2831@gmail.com

Papaver 15x21
Spontaneous watercolors are favorites of Irene ,
both to paint and to teach

IRENE… an accomplished artist whose diversity in mediums and subject matter allows her creative flexibility and provides patrons an impressive repertoire of her art.

She has traveled throughout the United States, Canada, Mexico, and Europe and lived in many of the regions, giving her a varied arena of subjects and inspiration. She attended universities in Colorado, California, and Arizona; has taken many art seminars and workshops. She attributes her professional art training to attending the Herzfeld School of Art in Wiesbaden, Germany.

Her work is included in many homes and businesses throughout the United States, Europe, Canada, and Mexico. Collectors are always made welcome at her home and studio in Chandler, Arizona.

All artwork ©

Alle-prima oil painting reflects realism as shown in the 'Night Intruder' – Oil 16 x 20

Irene's fondness for 'quakies' and skiing in Colorado inspired her pastel of the White Giants
20 x 28

Sunset Seascape – 28 x 28

Got Milk Cow – Acrylic 11 x 14

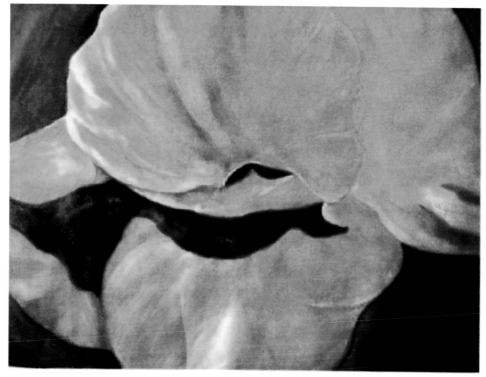

Hot Sauce – Watercolor 26 x 32

Quiet Water – Watercolor 25 x 31

Shaft of Gold – Watercolor 19 x 28

Irene's version of The Fruit Merchants by Estaban Murillo,
Oil in the 'old master-technique' 20 x 28

XI
Widow – Accepting Death & Beyond

It was 1991 when we purchased our lot and had our retirement home built at the Sun Bird Golf Resort community. However, we did not actually retire as Roland started preparing private income tax returns for people and I went full swing into teaching a variety of art classes at our community and other communities in the valley area. We did use our travel trailer to escape the hot summers and visited our family and friends until a few years prior to his heart issues. I continued doing my art teaching/painting murals and enjoying our 23 wonderful years at Sun Bird Community living with 'my frog', prior to his death on April 11, 2014.

He had had numerous heart-related health issues the last few years of his life but he still bounced back after each episode. He was due to come home in five days, after an open-heart surgery, when he suffered a massive heart attack while cuddled in my arms at the nursing center.

My *triple* trip to the altar was the best forty-two years of my life.

Today I am learning to spread my wings and trying to fly *SOLO* – but being a widow in a retirement community that has an abundance of widows has me reflect on Frank Sinatra's song, *'THAT'S LIFE'* ! It's not how fast or strong you start that counts—its how you finish.

Perhaps I shall spread my wings and 'fly again' before I call the control tower for landing permission to settle down upon *CLOUD SEVEN!*

As Ernest Hemmingway said, "It *is the journey that matters, in the end."*

ADDENDUM TO MEMOIR
'IF WE ARE STILL AN ITEM'
2017

I
A Bison Seduction

My neighbors informed me that a new widower, from the State of North Dakota, had recently purchased a home on the very next street and that I should contact him. Being the 'not so shy person' that I am I decided to do just that.

I knocked on his front door and could see him through the screened door at his back patio. He did not hear the doorbell and I suddenly felt shy – really me? – so I walked away – but only a few steps when I decided to go around the house and approach him at his back patio where he was having an afternoon 'libation' after his golf game.

I introduced myself with 'ruse' of saying, *"Is that your golf cart with the BUFFALO metal sign on it?"* Wherein he replied with a chuckle and the cutest grin showing his dimples, *"You obviously are not from North Dakota 'Sweetie", the pronunciation is 'BIZON'!"* I quickly replied, *"Well I may not be from North Dakota but I do know that Bison is spelled and pronounced with an 's' sound!"* and added that I was interested in obtaining a template of his 'Bison' sign for a painting I was currently painting. He then asked me if I would care to join him in a drink and I replied, *"Oh no, I don't drink hard liquor."* He then answered with a chuckle, *"How about a glass of wine?"* I quickly responded with my best smirked smile and nod as I sat down by his patio table.

We ended up talking for nearly two hours when I realized that I should go home when he let me know that I could use his 'Bison' sign IF I would paint him a 'Bison Head' of his North Dakota State alma mater emblem. I replied, *"Sure, anytime"*, then departed his place, walking 'on cloud 9', around the corner to my house feeling just fine!

I was able to observe my 'Bizon Buddy' over my backyard fence and noticed a day later that he was sitting out front of his place on patio chairs with a woman next to him. I felt quite disappointed that I was obviously too late in my attempt of seducing him! I found out later that the woman was his sister who was visiting him.

I decided to go ahead and hurriedly painted a large – 16" x 20"– oil of a Bison landscape just in case he should happen to grace my doorstep. I didn't want him to think I was a liar about my need for his Buffalo template!

A week passed when my doorbell rang and there was the 'dimpled' smiling guy with his "Bizon' emblem in hand asking IF I was still agreeable to paint his emblem. I, of course, said, *"Sure"*, and then quickly asked him if he'd care to observe some of my paintings and if he had time for a drink?

The 'seduction' worked and two days later we got really acquainted in his bedroom! The 'Bizon rutting season' continued with gusto, on both parts, to the point by the end of the winter season, when he was ready to return to his northern residence, he asked me if I was interested in going north with him. I decided to give the invitation a try, rather than remaining in the extreme summer heat months where I had endured alone for the last three years of widowhood, and agreed to the temporary venture.

II
The Trip North

Two months and seven days later we departed on the travel plans heading north via a sight-seeing venture through states he had not traveled before. Four hours out on the trip he commented, **"If we are still an item**...*I'd enjoy being with him on his pontoon boat"*...then he added, *"You do know how to swim, don't you?"* giving me one of his sexy, dimpled grins as I inquired about if he had life jackets on his boat! Right after that verbal exchange a song came over his car radio of the song, "Me and Mrs. Jones (my maiden name) – we got a thing going on... it is much too strong to let it go...". I just had a private laugh to myself thinking 'nothing ventured – nothing gained!'

I thought – here I go again –taking a chance on love and I barely know him – even though we met 82 days ago and now here I'm in his 'rag-top' convertible heading north on a planned one plus month vacation trip!

Being 'double again' is only an expression that applies to my past and present. I am definitely not interested in any permanent or legal connection but I am certainly enjoying being 'hooked-up' with this fun-loving-considerate-thoughtful-jovial-well-mannered-humorous – very sexy gentleman. I could add a lot more adjectives (than eight) to describe 'my squeeze' whom I shall refer to as my 'Bison Buddy'.

Friends ask me how I met my 'Bison Buddy' and I just grin and say *"I seduced him!"* In a way it was a 'mutual seduction'. He told his inquirers that I was too old to be seduced, but that I was 'very hot to trot!' It only took a few days later when the fire started and it has burned quite hot ever since he 'lit his torch!'

III

The Status

"Oh gosh, that song just came on again over the car radio –'Me and Mrs. Jones, we got a ting going on… my Baby does it good!" Once again, I am smiling to myself thinking of my maiden name – JONES – and my memoir that I had just completed before meeting my Bison Buddy.

In summation, my memoir – titled *80 Shades of Red* explains my start in life being in a double status – because of being a twin – and for those reasons I've always seem to be coupled with another.

"Am I headed back into the 'DOUBLE' status once again? I keep giving thought to his comment, *"IF we are still an item"* as I question myself as to what in the world am I doing here? Then, I sit back and try to relax in the 'speeding rag-top car' thinking oh well – *'here I go again, spreading my wings and 'flying' across the countryside with my 'Bison Buddy'!*

At least I am not in that 'solo status' as I was before meeting my 'Bison Buddy'!

IV
Bison Buddies

I enjoy writing so I kept a daily journal of the trip north with my 'Bison Buddy'.

We headed north from the Phoenix, Arizona area to Lake Powell area that 'BB' had not seen before and we enjoyed our first night together on the trip. It definitely was a 'three-star motel' experience.

Our second day out on this 'get-acquainted-adventure' we headed in the direction of Las Vegas, Nevada as BB had obtained tickets to attend the Celene Dion show the following day.

We stopped along the way and visited friends of mine that I had not seen for twenty years. I was a bit apprehensive about introducing my new 'friend' and concerned as to our 'non-marital + travel status'. As I suspected, BB just went with the flow and the introduction and brief visit was very comfortable and enjoyed by each of us.

This 'addendum to my memoir' could be considered as an 'advice guide' to the solo widows/widowers who are tired of sitting home alone – doing crossword puzzles or watching TV.

Arriving Caesars Palace we enjoyed something to eat and then the musical performance. Celene's song lyrics really touched sensitive feeling and once when

BB squeezed me I was pleased, then for a moment gave thought as to what were his feelings at that time? Were they for me or someone in his past? I then thought it probably is only natural for widows or widowers to have reoccurring thoughts/feelings of former times and I should 'shake off my uncertainty' and enjoy the moment. I did and the rest of the evening was also a 'star performance!'

Day four, of this travel adventure, we crossed the Death Valley route as BB had not seen the area before. We stopped for gasoline and something to eat and when we were standing at the gas pump I noticed a red-flashing-neon sign on the building extension of the restaurant that showed two cats with arched backs facing each other. Above the cats was the sign 'CAT HOUSE' and below that another flashing sign –'LADIES BROTHEL – FREE TOURS'! I started laughing and asked BB, *"Have you ever been in a 'cat house' before?"*

He just gave me one of those 'dimple grins' and I assumed that was possibly a 'yes grin' having remembered in our earlier conversations that he was a 'sailor' serving in the US Navy. I suggested that we take the 'free tour' as I was curious about the place.

BB rang the button, by the red door, and a large woman of color answered immediately showing a toothy grin as BB said, "*My Sweetie is looking for a job so we thought we'd take your 'free tour'!*" The jovial Madam opened the door and welcomed us inside laughing quite exuberantly, as did an elderly – also over-weight – gentleman (who was counting money at the single stool bar by the entryway). Both of them appearing to be quite amused at my embarrassment.

I quickly quipped, *I was hitch-hiking along the desert highway when my friend here picked me up so now I am really too tired right now to sign up for a 'trick'!*" We enjoyed the short – but interesting – tour and departed the area laughing as hard as the 'Cat House' personnel.

Day five of the sojourn, traveling along highway #195, our plan was to travel California Highway 120 to see Yosemite, as BB had not been there before, but the route was closed but to recent snow and poor road conditions. We then moved on spending the next night at South Lake Tahoe, California area. It was a nice area plus a nice evening!

The following day we ventured on, traveling via Highway 50, westerly in direction of the Napa Valley wine country area. The heavy snow fall and winter road conditions, along the coastal Highway #1, also caused several roadside slide challenges that did not seem to faze my chauffeur at the wheel of his convertible. His 'cruising' at rather high speeds at times had me quite concerned as to how to control my composure and appear to be relaxed and happy sitting next to him.

I certainly had had previous considerable road travel experiences having spent three solid years on many – sometimes difficult – roads in Europe traveling in an auto – then another six years living 'on the road' in a travel trailer – plus another twenty years of each summer – for three-months spells – again on the road traveling in a motor-home along many of the same highways we were now 'flying' in his convertible but NEVER at such high rate of speed! I began to give though as to what had I truly stepped into and IF I would even survive alive at the intended destination?

We still had to travel up the rest of the coastal route to the Pacific Northwest and then on to his North Dakota and Minnesota states. Also, I kept remembering his comments to me of how I would enjoy his pontoon boat rides and the 'smirk smiles' each time he asked, *"You do know how to swim, don't you?"* And then recalling his 'chuckles' when I inquired about any lifejackets aboard his pontoon! I put all those thoughts into my back pocket and decided I'd meet those challenges when, or if, we arrived at his lakeside property – that is– ***"If we are still an item!"***

V
Meeting My Family

When we reached the Seattle, Washington area our first 'family introduction' was with my daughter and a friend of hers. That was enjoyable as we toured the Pike's Market and waterfront area then some of the city sites before heading on south to the area where my twin sister lives.

I knew my daughter, Diane, would approve of my 'Bison Buddy' but I was a bit concerned about my twin's acceptance of him. We headed south to Ilene's farm and he charmed her over immediately. We spent several nights at her home. My twin was widowed two years before I was 'solo' again and she definitely would NEVER become involved with someone else as I have!

The second day we went to our other sister's home to meet more family members. Ilene was very nervous when he drove her car fast as he chauffeured us to our other sister's home seven miles away. I tried to reassure her that he was a safe driver but did not reveal that my own concerns matched hers!

Meeting and visiting my eldest living sister was quite a test for me and definitely for my Bison Buddy. Reason being is that our head count consisted of me, two sisters, a sister-in-law plus three of my nieces and the only 'Man of the Hour'. He charmed them all and did not seem to be phased by the inspection social event! Later when he drove my twin's car back to her house, as she and I sat in the back seat clutching each others 'sweaty hands', I whispered to her, *"Just pray – I know we'll be fine."*

We also visited close friends of his in the area north of Seattle and now it was my turn to be introduced to some of his long-time acquaintances.

I was very nervous although he assured me it would be fine. It ended up that his school chum's wife was also a twin, as charming, interesting and warm as family. They both made me feel most welcomed.

After spending eight days in the area we said our farewells to all and were back on the road again heading for North Dakota and Detroit Lakes, Minnesota.

Before closing this Addendum, I wish to add a **DOGGERAL** I wrote along this trip:

If We Are Still An Item

It Is Now Day Twenty-Two
I Am Not Even Blue
We've Gone From Single
To Becoming 'Two'
How Long Will It Last
Is Anyone's Guess
Meeting His Family
Will Be The Next Test
Seven Scenic States
We've Travelled So Far
Moving Along Swiftly
In His 'Rag-Top' Car
He Manages To Observe
All The Sites And Curves
I'm Riding Shotgun
Writing To Sooth My Nerves!
I've Now Met His Family
That Turned Out Real Fine
He Cooks Our Dinner Most Every Night
I'm Being Spoiled, But Feeling Just Right!

VI
Closing

The summer in the Northern States went very fast and I truly enjoyed my unplanned extended stay. I met a lot of his numerous friends plus enjoyed the pontoon rides every evening without needing to use the 'holy lifejacket'! Enjoyed seeing fabulous sunsets plus a lot of the lakes in the area. I also enjoyed the experience of being on his sailboat where the lifejacket worked just fine!

The four months seemed to fly by but when the cool weather arrived I kissed my 'sweetie' farewell and flew home. His parting remark to me was,

"If we are still an Item, I'll see you in November."

November arrived along with my Bison Buddy and we both seem to have adjusted to our being together so much so that he rented out his home, on the next street from me, and he moved into my house!

In closing this 'Addendum', I think it is safe, at this time, to remove the supposition 'IF' from the expression and now say—

"WE ARE STILL AN ITEM"

ABOUT THE AUTHOR

Irene Jones Coatta has written several short stories of humorous and spiritual travel experiences. She has also written a novel, *The Six Months Proposal*.

By profession, Irene is an accomplished artist whose diversity in mediums and subject matter allows her creative flexibility and provides patrons an impressive repertoire of her art.

She has travelled throughout the United States, Canada, Mexico, and Europe, and lived in many of those places. These locales have provided her with a wide variety of subjects and inspiration for her art. She attended universities in Colorado, California, and Arizona; and has taken many art seminars and workshops. She attributes her professional art training to attending the Herzfeld School of Art in Wiesbaden, Germany.

Her works are found in many homes and business throughout the United States, Europe, Canada, and Mexico. Collectors are always made welcome at her home and studio in Chandler, Arizona.

Made in the USA
San Bernardino, CA
15 May 2018